i explore

SHARKS

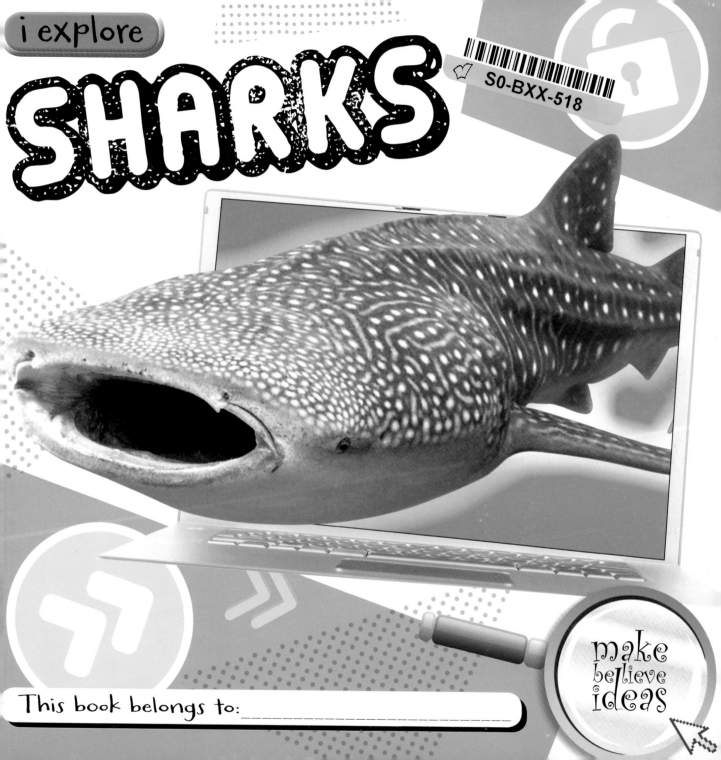

S0-BXX-518

make
believe
ideas

This book belongs to: _____

WHAT'S INSIDE?

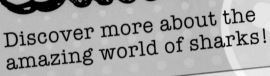

Discover more about the amazing world of sharks!

Sharks

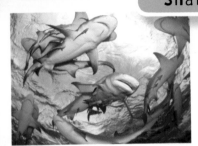

Hammerhead sharks

3-D

Throughout this book, you will find 3-D pictures to explore. Look for the 3-D glasses symbol to find them! To view the pictures, remove the 3-D glasses from the book cover and then hold the red lens over your left eye and the blue lens over your right eye. Watch as the picture comes to life!

Unusual sharks

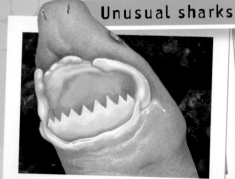

Great White Shark

Whale Shark

Silvertip Shark

Blacktip Reef Shark

Endangered sharks

i explore more & index

i explore

SHARKS

Amazing sharks live all around the world. There are about 450 types of sharks, including the gigantic Whale Shark, the spotted Zebra Shark, and the unforgettable Great White Shark.

Zebra Shark

i learn

Sharks use their fins to move in different ways: the tail fin pushes the shark forward; the pectoral fins help the shark to steer through the water; and the dorsal fin helps the shark to balance.

tail fin

Most sharks have dark-colored skin on the top half of their body, while their underside is a pale color. A dark color helps them blend in to the water when seen from above, while a pale color helps them blend in to the sky when they are seen from below.

dorsal fin

torpedo-shaped body

pectoral fin

i facts

A shark's skeleton is made of cartilage, which is much lighter than bone. This makes them fast swimmers.

The Thresher Shark's tail fin can grow up to 10 ft (3 m) long. For most Thresher Sharks, the tail fin is about as long as their whole body!

Thresher Shark

GREAT WHITE SHARK

snout

With its super-sharp teeth and powerful body, the Great White Shark is an excellent hunter. Like all sharks, the Great White uses all of its senses to hunt and catch its prey, including the ability to sense electricity!

i facts

i Sharks don't chew their food – they swallow it whole or in large chunks!

When a shark is about to attack, it will sometimes hunch its back, lower its pectoral fins, and swim in zigzags.

Shark ready to attack

ampullae of Lorenzini

→ i learn ✕

When a creature moves, its muscles give off electricity. Sharks can sense this electricity using tiny holes found on their head and snout. These holes are called *ampullae of Lorenzini*.

tooth

i discover

A shark's teeth are arranged in rows. When a tooth falls out, another tooth moves forward to replace it. The shape of a shark's teeth depends on the food it eats.

Megalodon Shark tooth

WHALE SHARK

teeth

The Whale Shark is a filter-feeding shark. It has around 350 rows of tiny teeth, but it does not use them for biting or chewing food. Instead, it sucks water into its mouth and then pushes it out through its gills, trapping any food in its gill plates.

 i discover

All filter-feeding sharks are slow swimmers. The Basking Shark moves at around 2.5 mph (4 kph), which is slower than a human walking!

Basking Shark

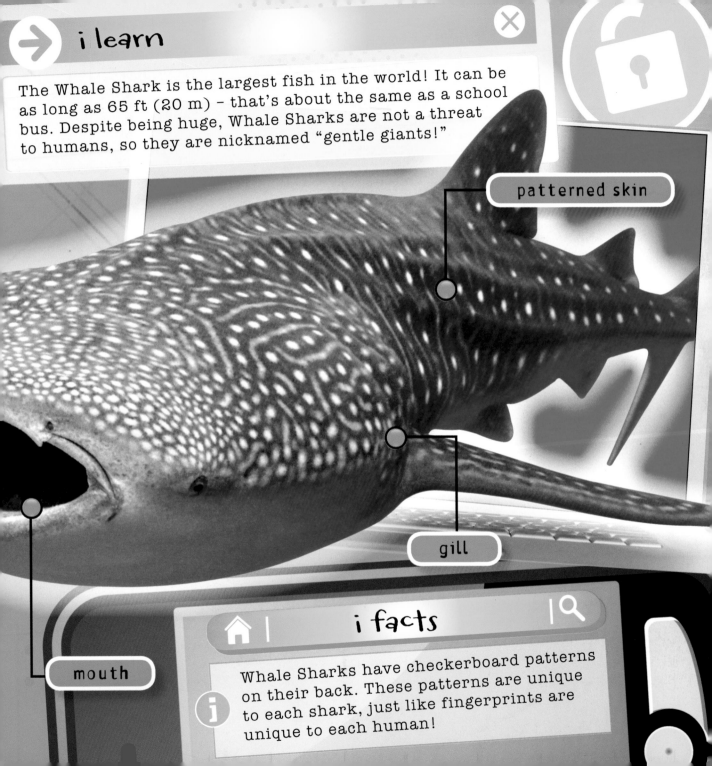

The Whale Shark is the largest fish in the world! It can be as long as 65 ft (20 m) – that's about the same as a school bus. Despite being huge, Whale Sharks are not a threat to humans, so they are nicknamed "gentle giants!"

patterned skin

gill

mouth

i facts

Whale Sharks have checkerboard patterns on their back. These patterns are unique to each shark, just like fingerprints are unique to each human!

HAMMERHEAD SHARKS

The hammerhead shark takes its name from its hammer-shaped head! This unusual head cuts through the water, making it easier for the shark to change direction as it swims.

i facts

i Some sharks have such a strong sense of smell, they could sense just one drop of blood in a swimming pool full of water.

Hammerhead sharks can get a tan! This happens when they have been in shallow waters or near the surface of the sea for a long time.

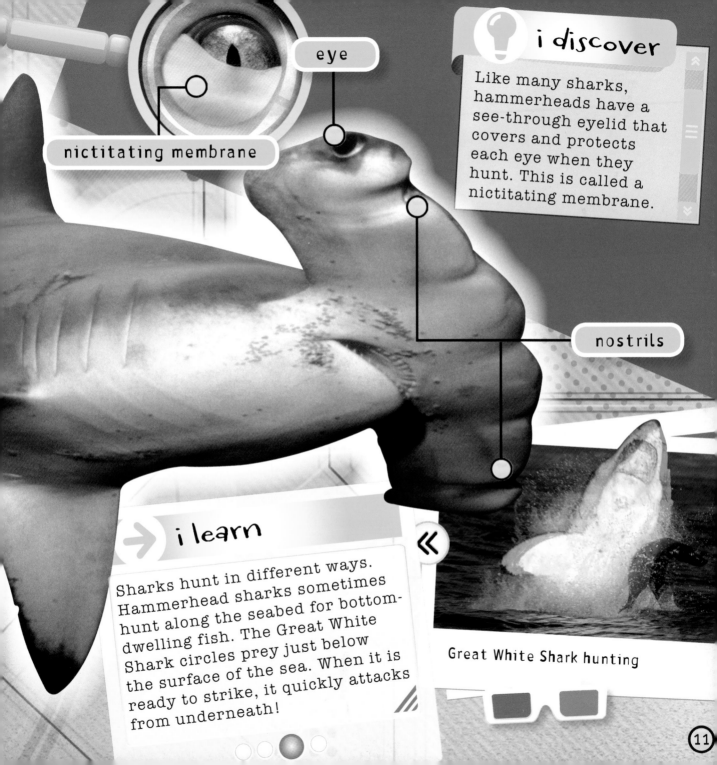

nictitating membrane

eye

i discover

Like many sharks, hammerheads have a see-through eyelid that covers and protects each eye when they hunt. This is called a nictitating membrane.

nostrils

i learn

Sharks hunt in different ways. Hammerhead sharks sometimes hunt along the seabed for bottom-dwelling fish. The Great White Shark circles prey just below the surface of the sea. When it is ready to strike, it quickly attacks from underneath!

Great White Shark hunting

SILVERTIP SHARK

mother shark

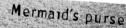

Different sharks have their pups in different ways – some sharks lay eggs, while others, like the Silvertip Shark, carry their pups inside them. As soon as a shark is born, it is left to fend for itself.

⌂ | i facts | 🔍

i Most sharks grow up with a natural instinct for hunting, which means they know how to hunt without being taught.

An empty shark egg is called a mermaid's purse.

Mermaid's purse

pup

While a Silvertip Shark pup is inside its mother, it is connected to its mother by a cord. This cord gives the pup food and oxygen. When the pup is born, the cord breaks and the pup swims away.

Bullhead shark's egg

✕

i discover

Mother bullhead sharks lay a soft, spiral-shaped egg. They push the egg between rocks, where it will be safe. The egg becomes hard over a couple of hours, and the baby shark grows inside it and hatches up to a year later.

Bullhead shark hatching

BLACKTIP REEF SHARK

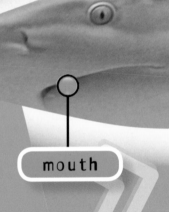

Just like humans, sharks need oxygen to survive. The Blacktip Reef Shark must keep water flowing over its gills to "breathe." To do this, it swims constantly. If it becomes trapped, it cannot pass enough water over its gills and can die.

mouth

gills

i learn

Sharks "breathe" by taking in water through their mouth and pushing it out through their gills. The gills take in oxygen from the water, and this oxygen is then carried around the shark's body by its blood.

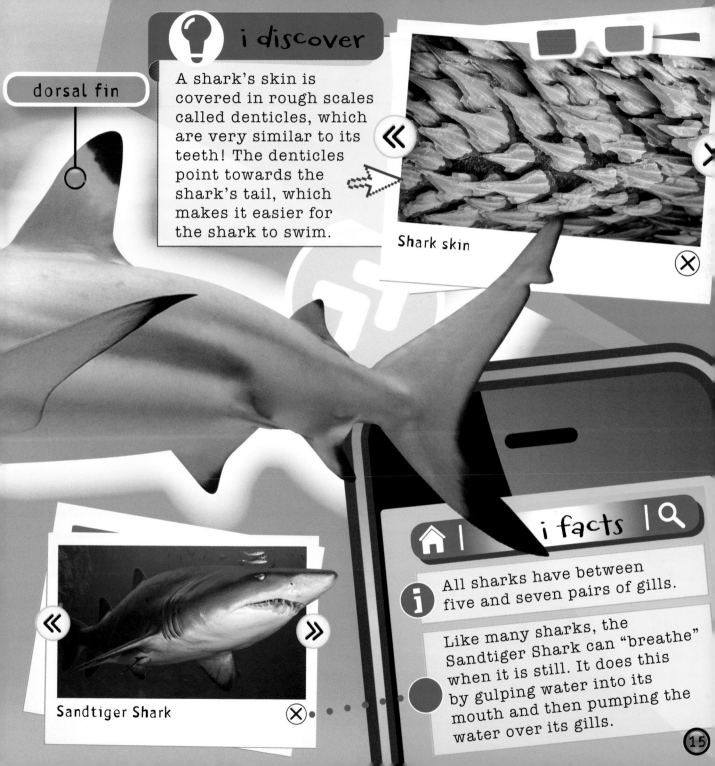

dorsal fin

i discover

A shark's skin is covered in rough scales called denticles, which are very similar to its teeth! The denticles point towards the shark's tail, which makes it easier for the shark to swim.

Shark skin

i facts

All sharks have between five and seven pairs of gills.

Like many sharks, the Sandtiger Shark can "breathe" when it is still. It does this by gulping water into its mouth and then pumping the water over its gills.

Sandtiger Shark

UNUSUAL SHARKS

All sharks have a skeleton made of cartilage, many rows of teeth, five to seven pairs of gills, and skin covered in denticles. Some sharks do not look like sharks at all – but they still belong to the shark family because they have these features.

mouth

whiskers

i learn

The Tasseled Wobbegong Shark has a beard of whiskers that look like seaweed or coral. The beard camouflages the shark so it can attack and eat small fish that come close!

Saw Shark

Saw Sharks have a long, blade-like snout that has teeth along the edges. They use it to kill their prey!

The smallest shark species in the world is the Dwarf Lantern Shark. It only grows to 6 in (16 cm) long. That's about the size of an adult's hand!

Tasseled Wobbegong Shark

Dwarf Lantern Shark

i discover

The Cookiecutter Shark takes its name from the cookie-shaped holes it leaves in its victims. It does this by sucking onto the prey with its lips, then cutting out circles of flesh.

Cookiecutter Shark

ENDANGERED SHARKS

Many sharks are in danger of becoming extinct. This means that the number of these sharks in the wild is falling and they might die out completely.

Great White Shark

i facts

Every year, humans kill up to 70 million sharks. On average, sharks kill fewer than 10 people each year.

The Great White Shark is famous for being the most terrifying shark of all, but its numbers are dropping due to human actions!

i learn

Sharks are hunted and killed by humans for their fins. After its fins are cut off, a shark is thrown back into the sea, where it dies. The fins are then sold for shark fin soup or to make traditional medicines. Although finning is banned in many countries, it still happens.

Shark fins

Hammerhead shark without fins

i discover

The Megalodon Shark lived 1.5 million years ago! This shark looked very similar to the Great White Shark, but it could grow up to 82 ft (25 m) long, which is longer than a truck! The Megalodon is thought to be the biggest shark that has ever existed.

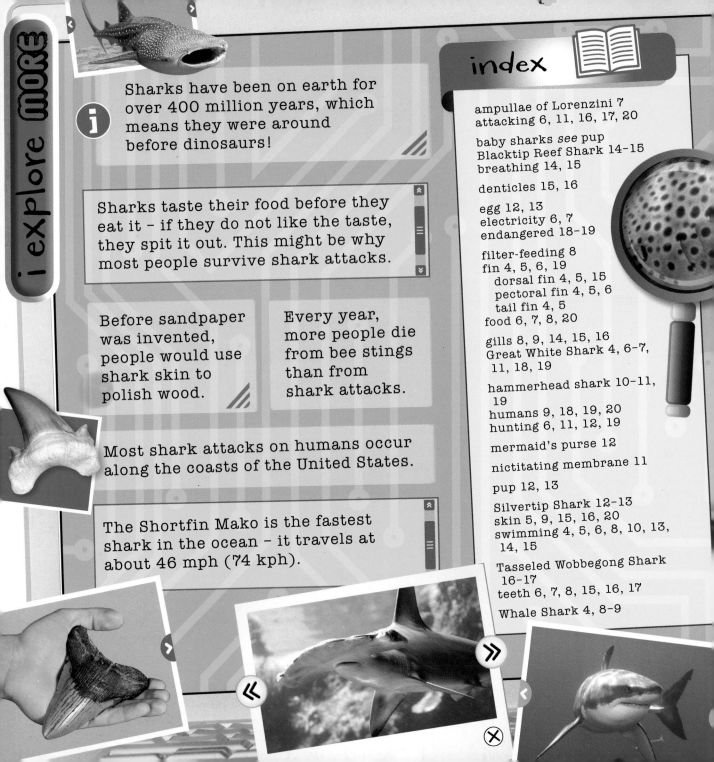

i explore **MORE**

ⓘ Sharks have been on earth for over 400 million years, which means they were around before dinosaurs!

Sharks taste their food before they eat it – if they do not like the taste, they spit it out. This might be why most people survive shark attacks.

Before sandpaper was invented, people would use shark skin to polish wood.

Every year, more people die from bee stings than from shark attacks.

Most shark attacks on humans occur along the coasts of the United States.

The Shortfin Mako is the fastest shark in the ocean – it travels at about 46 mph (74 kph).